save the . . .
BLUE WHALES

by **Christine Taylor-Butler**
with an introduction
by **Chelsea Clinton**

PHILOMEL

Dedicated to young readers everywhere.

Remember to dream big.

You are the key to saving our planet.

PHILOMEL BOOKS
An imprint of Penguin Random House LLC, New York

First published in the United States of America by Philomel Books,
an imprint of Penguin Random House LLC, 2023

Text copyright © 2023 by Chelsea Clinton

Photo credits: page 2: © NOAA Photo Library; page 5: © Sean Hastings/NOAA Photo
Library; page 9: © Izzet Noya/Adobe Stock; page 11: © Darin Sakdatorn/Adobe Stock;
page 14: © Darin Sakdatorn/Adobe Stock; page 23: © Emoji Smileys People/Adobe Stock;
page 26: © Dinal Samarasinghe/Adobe Stock; page 29: © mattbuck/Wikimedia Commons;
page 38: © Betty Sederquist/Adobe Stock; page 40: © Superstock/Adobe Stock; page 43:
© Luis/Adobe Stock; page 46: © Ivonne Wierink/Adobe Stock; page 58: © adfoto/Adobe
Stock; page 65: © Image No. SIA_000095_B44_F21_007/Smithsonian Institution Archives;
page 69: © coward_lion/Adobe Stock; page 72: © David J. Shuler/Adobe Stock

Philomel Books is a registered trademark of Penguin Random House LLC.

Visit us online at penguinrandomhouse.com.

Library of Congress Cataloging-in-Publication Data is available.

Printed in the United States of America

ISBN 9780593404140 (hardcover)
ISBN 9780593404157 (paperback)

1st Printing

LSCC

Edited by Talia Benamy and Jill Santopolo
Design by Lily Qian
Text set in Calisto MT Pro

The publisher does not have any control over and does not assume any
responsibility for author or third-party websites or their content.

save the . . .

save the . . .
BLUE WHALES

save the . . .
ELEPHANTS

save the . . .
FROGS

save the . . .
GIRAFFES

save the . . .
GORILLAS

save the . . .
LIONS

save the . . .
POLAR BEARS

save the . . .
TIGERS

save the . . .
WHALE SHARKS

Dear Reader,

When I was around your age, my favorite animals were dinosaurs and elephants. I wanted to know everything I could about triceratopses, stegosauruses and other dinosaurs that had roamed our earth millions of years ago. Elephants, though, captured my curiosity and my heart. The more I learned about the largest animals on land today, the more I wanted to do to help keep them and other endangered species safe forever.

So I joined organizations working around the world to support endangered species and went to our local zoo to learn more about conservation efforts close to home (thanks to my parents and grandparents). I tried to learn as much as I could about how we can ensure animals and plants don't go extinct like the dinosaurs, especially since it's the choices that we're making that pose the greatest threat to their lives today.

The choices we make don't have to be huge to make

a real difference. When I was in elementary school, I used to cut up the plastic rings around six-packs of soda, glue them to brightly colored construction paper (purple was my favorite) and hand them out to whomever would take one in a one-girl campaign to raise awareness about the dangers that plastic six-pack rings posed to marine wildlife around the world. I learned about that from a book—*50 Simple Things Kids Can Do to Save the Earth*—which helped me understand that you're never too young to make a difference and that we all can change the world. I hope that this book will inform and inspire you to help save this and other endangered species. There are tens of thousands of species that are currently under threat, with more added every year. We have the power to save those species, and with your help, we can.

Sincerely,

Chelsea Clinton

save the . . .
BLUE WHALES

CONTENTS

-- -- -- -- -- -- -- -- -- -- -- -- -- -- -- -- --

1

BENEATH THE OCEAN'S SURFACE

Imagine you had to find the biggest animal on the planet. You might be tempted to look for an elephant. If you did, you'd be close! Elephants are the biggest animal living on dry land. But they aren't the biggest animal on Earth. Where else could you look? In the water, of course! If you were to look, you would discover many creatures living beneath the surface. But only one animal qualifies for this assignment. You need to look for a blue whale.

Blue whales are the largest animals on Earth.

Have you ever seen a blue whale up close? They're almost ten times longer than the largest elephant. In fact, blue whales are the largest animal to ever have lived on planet Earth. They're much too big to swim in a lake, stream, or pond. They aren't found in large shallower waters like the Mediterranean or Red Seas. Blue whales need an enormous body of water to survive.

Luckily, our planet has plenty of deep oceans.

They cover about 70 percent of Earth's surface. That's almost 140 million square miles of water. More than enough space for blue whales to swim in! You'll find whales in every ocean except the Arctic Ocean. So finding a blue whale would definitely be exciting, but because the ocean is so vast and deep, it's not easy to do.

Whales Move Around!

Blue whales don't stay in one place all year round. They migrate. That means they change locations when the seasons change, to find food or to mate. A scientist once tracked a blue whale as it migrated. It traveled almost 1,600 miles in a single month. That's about as far as driving from Los Angeles, California, to Kansas City, Missouri!

Their favorite food, krill, thrives best in cold

polar regions at the northern and southern tips of the planet. Blue whales swim to those waters in the spring and summer. In the winter, the water becomes much too cold. So blue whales move back to warmer climates closer to the equator. That's where they breed and have baby whales, called calves. When the weather changes, the whales go back to their feeding grounds. Migrations take about four months in each direction.

Even with all that moving around, blue whales mostly swim alone. If you're lucky, you might see a few blue whales swimming in the same area. That happens when they are breeding and feeding their babies. If there is plenty of food in the area, they might join together in small groups called pods, but that is very rare.

So where would you even start to look for

Two blue whales in the Santa Barbara Channel.

a blue whale? That depends on which type of blue whale you want to find!

Southern Hemisphere Blue Whales

You'll discover three types of blue whales in the southern hemisphere. That's the southern half of the planet below the equator. Antarctic blue whales swim in the oceans near Antarctica each summer. Then they travel north toward the equator in the winter. Scientists call them "true" blue whales. They're a lot larger than all the other types of blue whales. Scientists aren't sure why.

Pygmy blue whales are the smallest of all the blue whale subspecies. They don't travel as far south as Antarctica. They stay mostly near Madagascar, the coast of Kenya, the Seychelles, and the southern Indian Ocean.

In 1970, scientists discovered a blue whale that wasn't like any of the others they'd seen. The whales were feeding off the coast of southern Chile, so they are known as Chilean blue whales. They're smaller than Antarctic blue whales but bigger than pygmy blue whales. They feed from December to May. After that, some of them travel to waters near the Galápagos Islands for the winter.

Northern Hemisphere Blue Whales

Northern blue whales live in the opposite hemispherc. And this is where things get a bit complicated. This subspecies has more than one habitat.

Some Northern blue whales live in the northern Pacific Ocean. So, of course, they're called North Pacific blue whales. Two separate populations are found from Alaska in North America to Costa Rica in Central America. But they don't migrate to the same places at the same time. So scientists call them the northeastern and northwestern populations. A popular place to see North Pacific blue whales is off the coast of California when they are feeding in summer and fall.

Other Northern blue whales live in the Atlantic Ocean. They're called North Atlantic blue whales. Blue whales that migrate from Canada to the eastern coast of the United States are called the northwest population. Blue whales that live near Iceland, the Azores Islands, and Norway are called the northeast population. Regardless of where they live, though, they all migrate south toward the equator in the winter.

There is one last subspecies to look for. Can you guess where you might find northern Indian Ocean blue whales? Near the northern Indian Ocean of course! Scientists believe they move during monsoon season, when there is a lot of hot, rainy weather.

Tons and Tons of Krill!

Blue whales can weigh four hundred thousand pounds or more! That's fifty times heavier than an average-sized elephant! All that weight means blue whales have to eat a lot of food to stay healthy. You might think that a blue whale would eat the largest ocean animal it could find. But a blue whale's throat is only four to eight inches wide. That's not big enough to swallow a big fish or other large animals. Instead, blue whales eat krill.

What are krill? They're tiny, shrimp-like animals living in the ocean. Krill swim in large

Krill look like tiny two-inch shrimp.

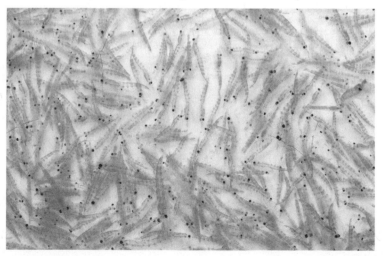

groups called swarms. Some swarms are so big they can turn the ocean red. If the swarm is big enough, astronauts can see it from space! That makes them easy for a hungry blue whale to find.

There's one problem, though. Krill are about two inches long. That's about the size of a paper clip. A blue whale may eat up to ten tons of krill each day. That's almost twenty thousand pounds of food. To do that, blue whales swallow up to two hundred gulps of krill each time they feed. Scientists estimate that each gulp contains 480,000 calories. You would have to eat 1,000 fish sandwiches or 2,500 cans of water-packed tuna to get the same number of calories. When a blue whale is finished eating for the day, it has consumed millions of calories. The average human adult only needs

Few humans have seen a blue whale up close.

two thousand calories a day to stay healthy.

Luckily, there are plenty of krill for whales to find in both hemispheres. Scientists estimate there are billions or trillions of krill living in all the oceans combined.

So here's a tip: if you want to find a blue whale, look for places where there are lots and lots of krill swarms!

2

EARTH'S GENTLE GIANTS

Despite their large size, blue whales are gentle and not a threat to humans. But because they're not easy to find, scientists don't know everything there is to know about them. In fact, humans walked on the moon before anyone ever studied a blue whale underwater. Most of what we know about blue whales is from studying whale bodies that have washed up on the shore. Luckily, blue whales can live up to eighty to ninety years. Their long lives give scientists lots of time to try to find and observe them in the vast oceans.

No Two Are Alike

You might be wondering how blue whales got their name. It's because they look light blue underwater. They're actually a patchy and uneven shade of bluish gray. The patterns on their backs and sides are unique, like a fingerprint, making it easier for scientists to tell individuals apart. Long ago, blue whales were called "sulphur-bottom whales." That name was even used in a famous book about a whale, *Moby-Dick*. That's because millions of yellow algae sometimes live on a blue whale's pale stomach and lower jaw. That makes their stomachs look yellow, which is the color of sulfur.

There is another way to tell blue whales

*Splotches on blue whale bodies
help scientists tell them apart.*

apart even when they are deep in the ocean.
Do you know how? If you guessed their songs,
you're right! Blue whales make one of the
loudest sounds on Earth. Their songs are so
loud their sound can reach 188 decibels. That's
louder than the engine of a jet plane, which
can reach 140 decibels. It's louder than rock

concerts, which can reach 135 decibels. It's so loud it would damage your ears if you heard it. But blue whales only sing underwater, which muffles the sound a bit, so you would be safe if you were nearby.

Sound travels in waves: the lower the frequency, the farther each wave can travel. Blue whales sing at a very low frequency, between fourteen and thirty hertz. That's fourteen to thirty sound waves per second. Blue whale songs can travel as far as one thousand miles. Scientists think blue whales use the sound waves to navigate when they're in deep dark waters. Or they may use them to communicate their location to other blue whales. And here's a fun fact: Only male blue whales sing using more than one note, and for up to twelve hours at a time! The males sing at night during the summer and during the day when they migrate in the winter. Scientists aren't sure why songs change with the seasons.

Born Big and Quickly Grow Bigger!

Unlike some animals, blue whales don't live in family groups. The mothers stay pregnant for about a year and have one baby at a time. Their babies are called calves. Because blue whales return to their breeding grounds in the winter, most calves are born between December and February.

Even though they're babies, newborn calves weigh up to six thousand pounds and can be twenty-three feet long. That's longer and heavier than many cars! Once a calf is born, the mother pushes it to the surface to take its first breath.

After that, the calves grow fast. They drink

sixty gallons of their mother's milk each day for about six months. All that milk helps them gain two hundred pounds in weight each day. By the time the calves are six months old, they're fifty feet long and weigh close to fifty thousand pounds. Contrast this with human babies who only grow to about sixteen pounds in that same amount of time (they usually start at around an average of seven pounds). Unlike human children, blue whale calves are ready to be on their own at six months. But they aren't mature enough to mate and have calves until they are between five and fifteen years old. Even then, the females only give birth every two to three years.

As Long as a Plane!

When a blue whale stops growing, it is very long. Blue whales in the southern hemisphere are 20 to 30 percent longer than blue whales in the northern hemisphere. For example, Antarctic blue whales stretch as long as 110 feet. That's about the length of a 737 airplane. Northern blue whales are closer to ninety feet long and weigh half as much as Antarctic blue whales. Pygmy blue whales are the smallest of the five subspecies, growing to an average of seventy to eighty feet. Even that is still pretty long. Females across all subspecies tend to weigh up to a hundred thousand pounds more than males. This may be because they need the extra weight and blubber to feed their calves.

Warm-Blooded in a Cold Ocean

You may not be as big as a whale, but you do have a few things in common with them. Whales are mammals, and you are too. That means your body is warm-blooded and can create heat to stay warm in cold environments. This is important since whales are not like fish. Most fish are cold-blooded, and their bodies adjust to match the temperature of the water. Objects in the ocean lose twenty-seven times more heat than those on land. Whales have to stay warm at all times, and creating heat uses up a lot of calories.

Luckily nature has a solution. Blue whales are covered in a layer of fat called blubber. It is thicker and has more blood vessels than the fat in your body. In fact, 27 percent of a blue whale's body is made up of blubber. The blubber helps the whale survive in cold ocean waters and stores nutrients for the whale to use in winter months when less food is available. It also helps explain why blue whales eat so much!

What Strong Backbones!

Another way blue whales are like you is that you're both vertebrates. That means you both have a skeleton with a backbone. Your skeleton supports your body and helps you stand upright on land even with the pull of gravity.

But blue whales don't live on land. Have you ever tried to float in the water? Did you notice how the water pushes up on your body and takes away some of the effect of gravity? This is called buoyancy. Buoyancy works the same way for whales. Their skeletons don't have to work as hard to support their enormous weight. And here's a fun fact: While you can both move your spine in a vertical direction (that's what you're doing when you're bending forward, for example), blue whales can't move their spine horizontally (which is what you're doing when you twist left to right). So a blue whale has to turn on its side to make a sharp turn.

Big-Hearted!

Like you, blue whales have a heart with four chambers. Their hearts are just much, much bigger. A blue whale heart weighs almost a thousand pounds and beats every two to thirty-seven seconds depending on how deep in the ocean the whale is swimming. When it does, it pumps as much as 1,400 gallons of blood through the whale's body. The aorta, a chamber in the heart, is so big you might be able to crawl through it. With the right equipment, you can hear a whale's heartbeat two miles away!

Fins, Flippers, and Flukes

Not everything about a blue whale's body is

like your body. Blue whales belong to a type of whale called rorquals. Rorquals have dorsal fins. The dorsal fins' main job is to help keep the whales from rolling over in the water the same way a keel on the bottom of a boat keeps it from tipping over. A blue whale's dorsal fin sticks out from its back and is about a foot long. No two dorsal fins have the same markings. That also helps scientists to tell individual whales apart.

Blue whales are part of a scientific group known as *Balaenoptera musculus*. *Balaenoptera* means "winged whale." *Musculus* means "muscle." Blue whales have lots of muscle but don't really have wings like their scientific name suggests. Instead, they have pointed flippers on each side of their bodies that are about eight feet long. The bones inside their flippers are similar to the bones in your hands. Blue

A blue whale's flukes are a rare sight!

whales use their flippers to swim and steer.

Here is another scientific word to learn: blue whales are part of a group of animals called cetaceans. Cetaceans are large marine animals that eat other animals and that use their strong tails to swim. You may have heard the word "fluke." It means to have a stroke of luck. But flukes are also the scientific name for a whale's tail. The blue whale's flukes are wide and thin with smooth edges and meet at a notch in the middle. They're almost twenty-three feet across and move up and down to help the whale move through ocean waters.

Seeing a blue whale's flukes is not common since they spend most of their time far from the shore and underwater. Plus, not all blue whales raise their flukes into the air when diving. So if you ever see a blue whale's tail rise from the ocean you can say it was "a fluke to see a fluke!"

What Big Eyes and Ears They Have!

Blue whales have eyes the size of grapefruits. But even though their eyes are big, they're not particularly useful for navigating when a whale dives into dark ocean water. Instead, blue whales rely on their excellent hearing.

Unlike human ears, every part of a blue whale's ear is inside its body. These ears are made of air pockets and bones and are filled with earwax. The bones detect sound vibrations. The wax helps carry sound to the whale's eardrum. A new layer of earwax forms every six months. You can use those layers to estimate a whale's age just like counting the rings in a tree. Based on these layers, scientists believe the oldest whale ever found lived for 110 years.

There They Blow!

Now take a deep breath. This fills your lungs with oxygen. If you went swimming, you would probably not be able to stay underwater for more than a minute or two. You would need to get more oxygen through your mouth or your nose. Whales have lungs too, but their lungs work better than ours. Blue whales can use up to 90 percent of the oxygen they take in. Our bodies use only 15 percent. Because of this, blue whales come up for air every five to fifteen minutes. If needed, they can hold their breath underwater for up to an hour.

A blue whale's blowholes are actually its nose.

When blue whales surface, they don't breathe through their mouths like people. That's because their mouth isn't connected to their lungs. Instead, blue whales breathe through two blowholes at the top of their bodies. That's the whale's nose. The holes can close when the whale dives deep. And blowholes are so big, a kid could crawl inside. But watch out! When it's time for the whale to blow out air, the spray can rise more than thirty feet!

A Giant-Sized Mouth!

Remember how much krill blue whales eat? It takes a lot of energy to catch them. So blue whales search for really big swarms and then dive beneath them. Suddenly, the whale speeds up toward the swarm, rolls on its side, and opens its mouth wide to let ocean water filled with krill pour in. Scientists call this lunge feeding.

The length of a blue whale's mouth and throat is almost a quarter of its entire body. When the whale eats, pleats inside the whale's throat expand like an accordion, creating a huge pouch. The pouch can hold one thousand pounds of water and krill with each gulp. Each gulp takes about five seconds. Then the whale pushes the water back out again for up to a minute. But how does the whale remove the water without losing the krill too?

Look inside your own mouth. You have teeth on the top and bottom of your jaw that help you chew your food. Blue whales don't have teeth. Instead, they have three hundred to four hundred plates called baleen that hang down from the top of their mouth. These

Baleen plates in a whale's mouth help filter water and krill.

bushy plates are made from keratin, the same protein your hair and nails are made of. Each baleen plate is several feet long and works the way a kitchen strainer might work when you drain water from cooked spaghetti. That's why blue whales are known as filter feeders. They use their large tongue to push the water out through the baleen plates. The krill remain trapped inside.

Stomachs That Get the Job Done

Once swallowed, the krill go down a tube called the esophagus. The esophagus is only four inches long and connects to the whale's stomach. You also have an esophagus that leads to your stomach, which has one chamber, but a blue whale's stomach has three: a forestomach, a main stomach, and a pylorus. Whales can't break down food by chewing the way you do. They swallow krill whole and let the chambers do the work.

Muscles in the forestomach squeeze to mash the krill. That chamber is full of bacteria that help break up the krill. Then liquids and acids in the main stomach turn the krill into nutrients. The pylorus passes the nutrients into the whale's intestines so they can be used by the whale for fuel. Whatever is left, including the krill's outer shell, gets ejected from the whale's body.

So Much Whale Poop!

You may know that farmers use cow manure (a fancy word that means poop) to fertilize their crops. You might even use it in your garden. But did you know that whale poop is a fertilizer for the ocean? It's true! Remember the krill that whales eat? The krill eat phytoplankton, a type of algae that grows in sunlight. Do you know what the phytoplankton needs to grow? Iron! What is full of iron? Whale poop!

This creates a continuous cycle. The krill eat phytoplankton. Whales eat the krill. The whales poop in the water. The phytoplankton gets its iron from whale poop. The krill eat the phytoplankton. And on and on it goes!

Other marine animals eat phytoplankton too, so whale poop is important. And blue whales create a lot of it. Almost fifty-three gallons of poop each time! So killing even one whale hurts the food chain that depends on it.

How did scientists figure this out? They studied places where a lot of whales had been killed. If those whales were no longer eating krill, the number of krill in that area should have gotten bigger. But the opposite happened. The number of krill decreased. Scientists realized that whale poop was important to maintain healthy ocean ecosystems.

An Unusual Way to Sleep

Do blue whales sleep? No! Can you believe it? Want to know why? When we sleep our brains automatically keep us breathing. But whales have to stay awake to breathe. If they didn't, they could drown. Because of that, a blue whale's brain needs to work differently from ours. When blue whales rest, buoyancy helps them float near the surface of the water. But only half of a blue whale's brain sleeps at one time so it can breathe and be alert in case of danger.

Fast, but Not Fast Enough

Blue whales swim about five miles per hour. But they can speed up to thirty miles an hour for a short time if they need to, especially if they see a krill swarm ahead. Their speed made them hard to hunt until boats became faster and weapons became more powerful.

When that happened, the lives of blue whales were changed forever.

THE HUMAN EQUATION

What makes our oceans so magical are all the diverse animals, plants, and other living things in them. Scientists estimate that we have only discovered a small fraction of the creatures living deep in their depths. So it's important that we keep them all safe.

The International Union for Conservation of Nature (IUCN) monitors the health of our planet and keeps a list of living things that need our attention. They call it the IUCN Red List of Threatened Species™. The list is grouped in seven levels of increasing danger.

Least Concern: These animals are doing well in their habitats.

Near Threatened: These animals are safe for now, but there are signs they may be in trouble in the future.

Vulnerable: These animals are at risk of extinction, but the risk is still low.

Endangered: The number of these animals is falling and they are losing large amounts of their habitat.

Critically Endangered: These animals have the highest risk of extinction in the wild. If we don't take action, these animals may disappear in the future.

Extinct in the Wild: The only places to find these animals are in sanctuaries and zoos.

Extinct: No more animals of this type are found on the planet.

Blue whales are listed as Endangered on the Red List. Scientists estimate that hundreds of thousands of blue whales lived in Earth's oceans in the 1800s. By 1960, 99 percent of Earth's blue whales were gone. The IUCN estimates there are only five thousand to fifteen thousand blue whales alive today.

The Antarctic blue whale is listed separately. It is Critically Endangered. There are only about two thousand still living in the wild today. That's only 1 percent of the number that lived decades ago. The good news is their numbers are increasing. But not fast enough.

So what's causing the problem? Apex predators. Those are the animals at the top of the food chain. They hunt other animals and have few natural enemies. Many large animals on Earth are considered apex predators, but blue whales are different. They're peaceful, and most animals leave them alone. But blue whales do have two enemies, and one is the most dangerous of all.

Killer Whales

Even though they are much smaller, orcas sometimes attack blue whales. These black-and-white marine animals are often called killer whales. So it might surprise you to learn that orcas are not really whales at all. They are actually the largest dolphins on Earth. Unlike blue whales, orcas have teeth, which makes them dangerous. Orcas hunt as a team. When they attack a blue whale, some might bite the whale's dorsal fin or tail to slow it down. Others might circle the whale to trap it. But blue whales are clever. They can flip and splash with their tail and swim away too fast for orcas to catch up. If they're looking for easier prey, orcas may follow mothers and calves to feeding grounds. They will try to separate a mother from her calf. Young calves are much easier to attack.

Even so, orcas aren't the only animal attacking blue whales. There is one apex predator that is much more dangerous.

Orcas will work as a team to attack other animals, including blue whales.

Human Hunters

Humans are apex predators too. And they're the main reason so few whales are left on the planet. How did that happen?

For hundreds of years, people have used whale meat for food and baleen to create stiffeners for products such as umbrellas and clothing. The oil in whale blubber was valuable for lighting lamps. In the past, the only way to get these materials was from sick or dying whales that washed up on shores. As early as the seventeenth century, though, whaling ships began hunting whales far out in the ocean to try to get more—and they succeeded.

But blue whales were harder to hunt than other whales. They were too big and too fast to catch with wind-powered boats and hand-tossed harpoons. They could also dive deep, making them hard to track in the water. So whalers mostly hunted smaller species of whales that came closer to shore. That all changed in 1868, when harpoon cannons were invented. The harpoons could hit large whales harder and from longer distances, making blue whales easier to catch.

By the late nineteenth century, steam-powered whaling ships were being built. These ships were faster and could travel farther, which

Powerful harpoon guns helped hunters hunt for bigger whales.

made it even easier to catch blue whales. By then, though, their baleen was no longer needed for consumer products. And blubber use decreased because petroleum had become a cheaper source of oil. The whaling industry struggled.

Then something happened. European countries, which had used blue whale fat to make soaps, now wanted to use it to make cheap substitutes for butter too. On top of that, glycerin in blue whale fat would soon become an important ingredient in explosives during World Wars I and II. Suddenly hunting blue whales became a big business again. The largest supplier of blue whale parts? Norway.

The Island Called Deception

When blue whale numbers decreased in the northern hemisphere, whalers looked for new places to hunt. One such place was Deception Island. The island is actually the top of an active volcano poking out of the Antarctic Ocean. The only way to reach its harbor is through a small passage.

Because Antarctica has twenty-four hours of sunlight in the summer, a lot of phytoplankton algae grows in those waters. Lots of phytoplankton means plenty of krill feeding on it. That makes Antarctica a popular destination for whales looking for big meals.

Once the word got out that there were lots of whales to be found there, ships from far away sailed to Deception Island too. They caught thousands of blue whales migrating to the feeding grounds. But the ships weren't large enough to handle all the whales they caught. To solve that problem, the Hektor Whaling Company built a town on the island in 1912. The town built large tanks to cook whale meat and a place to grind whale bones to use for fertilizer. Workers melted ice from nearby glaciers. The water was used to fill the boilers needed to turn blubber into oil. The town was nicknamed Whalers Bay.

By 1931, new ships were big enough to process whales. Whalers Bay was abandoned, but the damage continued offshore. More than 360,000 blue whales were hunted and caught

Old boiler tanks can still be found on Deception Island.

worldwide between 1910 and 1965. Almost all of them, at least 330,000, were killed near Antarctica.

You can still go to Deception Island to see Whalers Bay as a tourist. If you do, it might make you sad. The big rusting tanks and large whale bones sticking up from the beach remind visitors of what once happened there.

Other Ways Human Activity Hurts Whales

Ships Built to Carry Humans and Cargo

As modern ships became larger and faster, a new danger put blue whales at risk. The danger wasn't from hunting, but from accidental strikes by cruise ships, oil tankers, and freighters. When a huge ship hits a blue whale, it can be seriously injured or killed. Because these accidents happen far out in the ocean, researchers don't always find the bodies, so it's hard to get an exact count of how many whales are killed in this way. Instead, they have to estimate based on the whales they do find. For example, between 1988 and 2013, thirty whales washed up on the California shore. More than a third of the dead whales were killed by ships. So the true number is likely higher. Today, scientists record scars and injuries that they find on blue whales still living—whales that clearly got into ship accidents but survived—to determine how to better protect them.

Those large ships sometimes have other accidents that can put blue whales in danger. Thousands of gallons of oil may spill into the water. The oil pollutes the water and poisons the krill that blue whales need to eat. It can also irritate the whales' bodies, making them sick.

Inhaling toxic vapors from the oil may kill blue whales over time. And of course, oil spills don't stay in one place. The oil can travel with the ocean tides and expose more whales to the danger.

Fishing Nets

Even small boats can present a danger to blue whales. For example, sometimes fishing boats want to catch a lot of fish at one time. They use nets made of nylon to do it. Those strong nets can accidentally catch large marine creatures

Nylon fishing nets are strong enough to hurt blue whales.

too. If a net catches a blue whale, it can be dangerous in a number of ways. Blue whales can get trapped and not be able come up to the surface for air. If that happens, the whales could drown. The nets might also hurt their fins, flippers, and tails, making it harder for them to swim even if they escape. In 2021, a study estimated that 60 percent of the blue whales near the Gulf of Lawrence in Canada had been hurt by fishing nets.

Military Sonar

Humans can harm whales in other ways too. In some countries, the military conducts sonar experiments. Sonar uses sound waves to find large objects underwater. The sound waves bounce off the objects and echo back to the sender. That helps the military determine the size, shape, distance, and speed of those objects in the water. It helps submarines navigate in deep dark waters. It is how the military can tell if enemy submarines are nearby.

Testing sonar to make it better sounds like a good thing, right? For whales, it's not. Whales are large objects too. And as people discovered, the sonar tests hurt them.

In the 1990s, animal protection groups and environmentalists asked the US Navy to stop testing sonar because it was hurting whales. But the navy didn't stop the tests. In 2000, six small whales died on Bahamian beaches. Soon, other sick and dying marine animals were found as well. Some had bleeding ears. An investigation proved the navy's sonar was responsible. But there was no proof that sonar also hurt blue whales, which are much larger. Scientists and activists knew that they had to find more evidence.

To test their theory, scientists from Southern California attached tags to blue whales with suction cups to track them. Then they sent sonar waves into the water. The sonar the scientists used was much weaker than what the military used. The sound was even lower than the sound blue whales make on their own. When the sonar was used, the whales stopped eating or diving. Instead, they swam faster and moved away from the sound. The scientists finally had proof that sonar was hurting blue whales. Even so, the navy didn't stop their testing. They had to be sued.

In 2015, a federal court ordered the US Navy and the National Marine Fisheries Service to find ways to test their sonar that wouldn't hurt marine animals. They limited how many sonar tests the navy can do in waters near Hawaii or Southern California where blue whales are found. The restriction lasts until the year 2025.

Plastic Trash

Everyday actions by humans can hurt blue whales too. Sadly, the plastic you bring home from the store sometimes finds its way into the ocean after it is thrown away. It piles up in the water. Remember, blue whales eat by gulping in large amounts of water and krill. When they do this, they can accidentally gulp in trash that humans have left behind. There are more than five trillion pieces of plastic currently floating in the ocean. That includes plastic bags, soda can rings, packaging, and fishing gear. Plastic takes hundreds of years to decompose and break down to a point where it's no longer harmful. The plastic can get trapped by the baleen in a whale's mouth. Tiny pieces of plastic can get through to a whale's stomach and make it sick.

Another problem? Microplastics. They're found in everything from toothpaste and lotions to clothing. They sometimes wind up in the ocean as well. The plastic beads are smaller than a grain of sand. Microplastics can break down in the sunlight and poison the water. That hurts blue whales and the krill they eat too.

Climate Change

Here's one more thing that's hurting blue whales: climate change. Oceans are the largest ecosystem on the planet. Most life on Earth is in our oceans, and they are very much affected by climate change. Remember, ocean water absorbs heat from anything floating in it and from the atmosphere around it. That means when the planet's atmosphere is warming, the ocean is too. That heat changes the nature of a habitat.

Oceans absorb other things from the atmosphere too, like carbon dioxide gas. You probably know that too much carbon dioxide helps cause climate change. But did you know that it also makes ocean water acidic? When ocean water becomes more acidic, it makes it harder for krill to create the outer shell they need to survive. If the krill can't survive, there are less for blue whales to eat, which in turn makes it harder for the whales to survive.

Believe it or not, blue whales can actually help solve this problem. How? It all goes back to the feeding cycle. Phytoplankton absorbs carbon from the water. Krill eat the phytoplankton and absorb that carbon too. Whales then eat the krill. That carbon remains trapped in the whale's body. When the whales die, their bodies sink to the bottom of the ocean. This is called a whale fall. The bodies decay and release carbon dioxide gas back into the water over time. This provides nutrients for organisms living on the ocean floor. Did you know that the carbon released by all the whales that died each year before hunters reduced their numbers was estimated to be as high as 1.9 million tons? That's as much as is made by 410,000 cars.

By the way, blue whales are more important to ocean ecosystems than you might think. It's not just their poop and their ability to trap carbon that are useful—they also help circulate nutrients in the water. They eat, dive deep, and swim. This stirs things up throughout the vast ocean layers. As the whales swim, they spread their poop everywhere they go. This process is called a whale pump. By doing this, the whales help the ocean recycle nutrients in the water. Whale pumps send those nutrients back to the upper layers of the ocean where phytoplankton lives. More phytoplankton means more carbon can be captured from the atmosphere. This continues the feeding cycle.

That's why the planet needs to restore whale populations, including blue whales. Before they were hunted, whales removed as much carbon from our atmosphere as all the forests on the planet. On average, a single whale captures as much carbon as one thousand trees. But so many whales have been killed in the last hundred years that millions of tons of carbon are no longer being removed. The good news is that there are plenty of people working to save the whales. Let's find out more about them now.

MAKING A DIFFERENCE!

As you can see, whales are an important part of Earth's ecosystem as a whole. It will be hard to heal the planet if we don't increase the number of whales in our oceans. The good news is that blue whale populations are increasing— but not fast enough. If you want to help save blue whales, there are many great people who are working on just that. If you want to help save blue whales, here are some of the people and organizations doing this important work.

The International Whaling Commission

The International Whaling Commission (IWC) was created in 1946. The founders realized that huge numbers of whales (including blue whales) were being killed by commercial whaling. They wanted to focus on protecting whales and increasing their numbers. To solve the problem, they brought countries together to make new rules that would help.

At first, the IWC set limits on how many whales could be hunted by any given country. But the limits didn't work. More than one million whales were killed in the years that followed. So in 1966, members called for a total ban on hunting whales for commercial reasons. That means any reason designed to help people make money. Countries could only get permits to hunt whales for scientific reasons. Even so, the commission set strict limits on how many whales a country could take. Unfortunately, not all countries played by the rules. Two countries account for almost all whale hunting today: Norway and Japan.

Despite these obstacles, the IWC's plans to save whales are working. The number of blue whales on Earth is increasing! In 1966, only four hundred Antarctic blue whales remained. Today, there are almost two thousand. That is still less than 10 percent of the whales that existed before commercial whaling began, but it's a positive start.

The National Oceanic and Atmospheric Administration

The National Oceanic and Atmospheric Administration (NOAA) plays an important role in

*Responsible whale watch companies
can help you see whales from a safe distance.*

keeping all whales safe. Its scientists learn
about whale behavior and find ways to identify blue whales in the ocean. They create maps
of oceans where whales have been seen. This
helps boats avoid them. NOAA rescues injured
whales and removes whales that wash up on
beaches. It also studies noise in the ocean
that might harm or confuse the whales. To save
whales, NOAA manages two important laws.

The Marine Mammal Protection Act

(MMPA) forbids US citizens from taking, feeding, or bothering any marine mammals, including whales, in US waters and even farther out in the ocean. The MMPA also makes it illegal for anyone to import marine mammals or products made from them into the United States. The only exceptions are for scientific research, breeding programs, and hunting by indigenous Alaskans.

The government realized some animals need extra protection. So NOAA also manages the Endangered Species Act (ESA) with the US Fish and Wildlife Service. This law allows the federal agencies to create conservation programs to keep threatened animals safe. The agencies track and monitor the health of whales where possible and ask ships to reduce their speeds when whales are migrating. Scientists continue to look for ways to reduce noise pollution that causes whales to move away from their habitats. NOAA conducts a report on the status of blue whales every five years. The ESA lists blue whales as endangered. For now, that means their numbers are still very low.

Whale Sanctuaries

One of the best ways to protect blue whales is to create safe habitats, called sanctuaries, for marine animals. Sanctuaries are also excellent places to study whales when they are migrating. People are allowed to swim or visit by boat as long as they don't disturb the animals. Many sanctuaries have visitor centers where you can learn all about blue whales if you want to stay on land.

There are sanctuaries all over the world.

But in the United States, NOAA has a special department to oversee them. Its Office of National Marine Sanctuaries manages fifteen ocean sanctuaries and three national monuments across the United States and its territories. Here are two you can visit:

Channel Islands National Marine Sanctuary gets frequent visits from blue whales. It is located off the coast of Southern California about a hundred miles from Los Angeles. You can only get there by boat or small plane. The sanctuary covers 1,470 square miles of ocean water and five small islands. Remember the two North Pacific blue whale populations? Blue whales live in this sanctuary from February through October. They visit while migrating south to Mexico in the fall or north to Canada in the spring.

Northeast Canyons and Seamounts Marine

National Monument is located 130 miles off the coast of Cape Cod in Massachusetts. It was declared a national monument by President Barack Obama in 2016. Measuring almost five thousand square miles, it's as big as Connecticut! Other baleen whales, such as humpback whales, have been seen in the area over time. In February 2020, researchers from the New England Aquarium were excited to see blue whales swimming there too.

So if you want to see whales in the wild, sanctuaries are a great place to do so! Just be sure to check with the sanctuary before you go for the best time of year to visit.

People to the Rescue

Even with all of these great efforts, blue whales will still be in danger without more help. Luckily, there are lots of people who have made learning about whales a personal mission.

Dr. Sylvia Earle is a famous oceanographer who may be the first person to have seen a blue whale underwater. As a kid, she would go to museums and dream of seeing animals up close. She learned to scuba dive and spent more than seven thousand hours underwater. Here's how her passion helped the world learn more about blue whales. In the 1960s, the American Museum of Natural History in New York created a life-sized sculpture of a blue whale. Seeing a live blue whale was so rare that the museum had to use photographs and measurements of a whale that died in Europe in 1925. The sculpture was ninety-four feet long and was painted a dull gray. The museum had no idea that their finished model didn't look like a living blue whale in the wild!

Years later, Dr. Earle was studying humpback whales off the coast of Hawaii. Suddenly, a few curious blue whales swam alongside her team's boat and followed them. Dr. Earle was curious too. So she dove into the water and watched the blue whales swoop and twirl for two and a half hours. She was able to give the museum better information to redesign their sculpture. The whale was repainted and the flukes were changed in 2001. Twenty-eight hairs were added to the whale's chin, but they forgot to add a belly button. In 2003 that was added too. Dr. Earle's discovery made it possible for kids to see what blue whales look like up close. She is now the president of Mission Blue, an organization that works to protect and explore oceans. She was named "Hero for the Planet" by *TIME* magazine.

*The Smithsonian Institution created
this life-sized model of a blue whale in 1963.*

Dr. Nick Pyenson is the Smithsonian Institution's curator of fossil marine mammals. That means he's a whale detective who travels all over the world to study marine fossils and skeletons to learn about the history of whales over time. He's such a good detective that in 2011, he discovered skeletons of baleen whales in the dry Atacama Desert in Chile. As his team began to dig, they found more and more complete skeletons. It turns out the whales had once lived in an ancient ocean that had covered the area more than seven million years ago. Dr. Pyenson works for the National Museum of Natural History, which is part of the Smithsonian, in Washington, DC. The museum has the largest collection of whale bones, skulls, and fossils in the world! Their "whale warehouse" is as big as a football field and helps scientists like Dr. Pyenson learn how whales have changed over the last forty million years. Those bones also help him identify new species of whales when they are found. Dr. Pyenson has used his knowledge to write a book called *Spying on Whales: The Past, Present, and Future of Earth's Most Awesome Creatures*. He received the Presidential Early Career Award for Scientists and Engineers from President

Obama. How did Dr. Pyenson become interested in whales and fossils in the first place? His parents took him to natural history museums when he was a child, and that sparked his interest, of course!

Dr. Asha de Vos is a marine biologist in Sri Lanka. She also got her inspiration to help blue whales when she was a child. She saw a skeleton of a blue whale at a museum and thought the vast ocean was magical. Now she researches blue whales in the northern Indian Ocean. To help with this, she created Oceanswell, an organization that teaches the local community how to be better ocean guardians and how to protect whales. Oceanswell even has workshops to help kids create their own animated videos so they can teach other people about what they've learned about whales. Dr. de Vos also created

Ocean Hero Huddle, a monthly online discussion for kids to talk and share ideas about what they are learning. In 2020, Dr. de Vos was named Sea Hero of the Year. The award, sponsored by SEIKO, a Japanese watch company, honors divers who are on the front lines of ocean and marine-life conservation and helps them continue their important work.

More Foundations and Museums Making a Difference

As you've learned, many museums and foundations play an important role in helping kids learn more about blue whales and how to save them. Here are a few more that do the same.

The Natural History Museum in London has a blue whale skeleton made from real bones. They call this skeleton Hope. She is almost eighty-three feet long and weighs nearly five tons. Hope was found stranded in Ireland in 1891. Her bones were put into storage until 1934. That's when the staff put the bones together and hung her skeleton in the museum's Mammals Hall. In 2017, the museum moved her to a much bigger space. It took three weeks to label and remove all the bones before they could be transferred safely. If you visit, you can see Hope hanging from the ceiling of Hintze

A blue whale skeleton is on display at the Natural History Museum in London.

Hall. She is posed in a lunge-diving position as if she were ready to swallow krill.

The Pacific Whale Foundation (PWF) is located in Hawaii. They focus on protecting whale habitats by making the ocean healthier. Volunteers were able to get smoking banned on Maui beaches because cigarette butts were polluting the water. They also helped get plastic bags banned in Maui County and stopped high-speed ferry boats from traveling through waters where whales were having their calves. If you visit Hawaii, you can take one of their whale watch cruises to see whales in their natural environment. You can even learn about whales at their annual film festival!

The World Wildlife Fund (WWF) is another great resource. Remember the subspecies of blue whales discovered near the coast of Chile?

Researchers realized that large fishing companies and salmon farms were also using those waters, which increased water pollution in the whale's feeding grounds. Whales were also getting hit by boats in the area. To help solve this problem, the WWF tagged blue whales in that area and tracked them by satellite. The WWF then created maps to help people avoid the whales and keep them safe.

The American Cetacean Society (ACS) provides education and outreach on the conservation and protection of whales. They have student chapters that can help you learn about whales. They also have teaching guides you can use in your school. If you want to learn how to contact your elected officials and let them know that you're concerned about blue whales, the ACS can show you how to do it.

A blue whale swimming at the surface of the water.

Your Turn!

Now you know all the reasons why we need to protect blue whales. The health of our planet depends on it. Even though you live on land, you can help make a difference to save these majestic creatures.

FUN FACTS ABOUT BLUE WHALES

1. Female whales are called cows. Male whales are called bulls.

2. Blue whales may be affectionate and can form bonds with other animals.

3. The shape of a blue whale is similar to a submarine.

4. Baby whales are bigger at birth than almost every fully grown adult animal on the planet.

5. The milk from a blue whale contains 35–50 percent fat. Whole milk created by a dairy cow is only 3.5 percent fat.

6. Fully grown blue whales are almost as long as the Space Shuttle orbiter.

7. Blue whales have tongues and noses (which are their blowholes) but cannot taste or smell well.

8. The tongue of a blue whale weighs as much as a single elephant.

9. Blue whales might be the biggest whales, but they do not have the biggest brains. Sperm whale brains are larger.

10. Scientists have discovered eleven different song types used by blue whales.

HOW YOU CAN HELP
SAVE THE BLUE WHALES

You might be wondering, "What can I do to help blue whales?" The answer is: plenty of things! Here are just a few of them.

1. Ask the International Whaling Commission to keep blue whales on endangered lists. They are trying to keep countries like Japan, Norway, and Iceland from killing more whales. Even though blue whale numbers are increasing, there are still very few compared to a hundred years ago. When animals are removed from endangered lists, it's called delisting. Don't let this happen to blue whales.

2. Support organizations like the World Wildlife Fund that try to help blue whales. The WWF has tools and lessons for kids on their website, WorldWildlife.org, which can help you take action.

3. Ask an adult to download the Ocean Alert app. If you see a whale, you can use the app to report it. You can use the app to add details and even send a photo of what you saw. The app sends alerts to boats and sailors in the area so they can watch for whales.

4. If you see a whale in trouble, you can call 1-877-SOS-WHAL. This alerts the Coast Guard. If you are on a boat with

a very high frequency (VHF) radio, you can contact them on VHF channel 16.

5. If you go on a boat ride, make sure the driver is being safe. The boat should move slowly in waters where whales are spotted. Stay at least three hundred feet away from any whales that you spot. If you see someone violating the law, you can call the NOAA Fisheries Enforcement Hotline twenty-four hours a day at 1-800-853-1964.

6. Join the Break Free from Plastic movement and avoid single-use plastics. Plastics take hundreds of years to break down. If you use less plastic, there will be less to make its way into the oceans. You'll be helping the planet at the same time.

7. Write to your senator or representative. Ask them to keep funding the important work that NOAA does to keep blue whales and their habitats safe. You can find your representatives at Congress.gov /Members/Find-Your-Member.

8. Write a report about blue whales or make a video. You can also draw pictures showing what you've learned. Share them with your friends, family, and classmates. The more we can do to educate people about blue whales, the more blue whales we can save.

Many hands make light work. Together we can make a difference!

ACKNOWLEDGMENTS

To Ken, Alexis, and Olivia for encouraging me to dream big. And to my amazing assistant, Kim Parham, for pointing out the importance of whale poop!

REFERENCES

WEBSITES

American Museum of Natural History. amnh
.org/exhibitions/permanent/ocean-life
/blue-whale-model.

National Geographic Kids. kids
.nationalgeographic.com/animals
/mammals/facts/blue-whale.

National History Museum. nhm.ac.uk/bluewhale.

NOYO Center for Marine Science. noyocenter
.org/marine-mammals/blue-whales.

Smithsonian Institution. ocean.si.edu/ocean
-life/marine-mammals/whales.

ARTICLES

De Vos, Asha. "Why Are Blue Whales So Enormous?" TEDEd. ed.ted.com/lessons /why-are-blue-whales-so-enormous-asha -de-vos#digdeeper.

Sofia, Madeline K. "Travel Through Time with a Whale Detective." NPR. June 7, 2017. npr.org/2017/06/07/531112519/travel -through-time-with-a-whale-detective.

Welch, Craig. "Elusive Blue Whale Behavior Revealed by Their Songs." *National Geographic*. February 15, 2018. nationalgeographic.com/science/article /blue-whale-songs-behavior-decoded-spd.

Whale Watch Western Australia. "The Anatomy of a Blue Whale." April 2, 2020. whalewatchwesternaustralia.com/single-post /2020/04/02/the-anatomy-of-a-blue-whale.

CHRISTINE TAYLOR-BUTLER is the author of more than ninety fiction and nonfiction books and articles for children. A graduate of MIT, she holds degrees in both civil engineering and art & design. She has served as a past literary awards judge for PEN America and for the Society of Midland Authors. She is an inaugural member of steaMG, an alliance of middle grade science fiction authors, and a contributor to STEM Tuesday. She lives in Kansas City with her husband, Ken, and a cat who thinks he's a dog.

Photo by Kecia Y. Stoval

You can visit Christine Taylor-Butler online at
ChristineTaylorButler.com
and follow her on Twitter
@ChristineTB

CHELSEA CLINTON is the author of the #1 *New York Times* bestseller *She Persisted: 13 American Women Who Changed the World*; *She Persisted Around the World: 13 Women Who Changed History*; *She Persisted in Sports: American Olympians Who Changed the Game*; *Don't Let Them Disappear: 12 Endangered Species Across the Globe*; *It's Your World: Get Informed, Get Inspired & Get Going!*; *Start Now!: You Can Make a Difference*; with Hillary Clinton, *Grandma's Gardens* and *The Book of Gutsy Women: Favorite Stories of Courage and Resilience*; and, with Devi Sridhar, *Governing Global Health: Who Runs the World and Why?* She is also the Vice Chair of the Clinton Foundation, where she works on many initiatives, including those that help empower the next generation of leaders. She lives in New York City with her husband, Marc, their children and their dog, Soren.

Photo courtesy of the author

You can follow Chelsea Clinton on Twitter
@ChelseaClinton
or on Facebook at
Facebook.com/ChelseaClinton

DON'T MISS MORE BOOKS IN THE

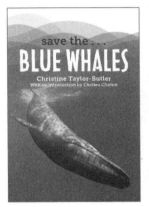

save the . . .
BLUE WHALES
Christine Taylor-Butler
With an introduction by Chelsea Clinton

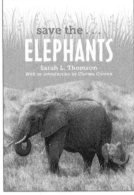

save the . . .
ELEPHANTS
Sarah L. Thomson
With an introduction by Chelsea Clinton

save the . . .
FROGS
Sarah L. Thomson
With an introduction by Chelsea Clinton

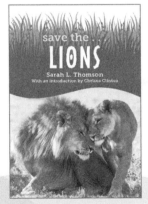

save the . . .
LIONS
Sarah L. Thomson
With an introduction by Chelsea Clinton

save the . . .
POLAR BEARS
Christine Taylor-Butler
With an introduction by Chelsea Clinton

save the . . . SERIES!

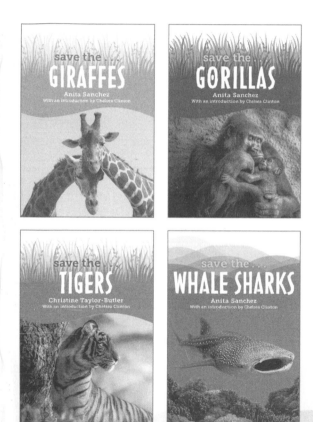